Life Winks

Inspirational Quotes for the
Risk Taker and the Adventurous Soul

Todd A. Hyndman

Copyright © 2015 Todd A. Hyndman

All rights reserved.

ISBN-10: 0692406557
ISBN-13: 978-0692406557

Edited by Carolyn L. Mears
Cover design by Tim Morris

DEDICATION

This book is dedicated to those of you who take risks, embrace challenges, set goals, seek adventure, and who make it a priority to improve your life. Each day should start with a positive thought. I hope you enjoy this book and never give up on your dreams!

Todd A. Hyndman

ACKNOWLEDGMENTS

I would like to thank my family and friends who believed in me and who supported me along the way. Your encouragement helped me push through all of the obstacles.

Todd A. Hyndman

The power of choice is life changing, so choose well.

Extraordinary lives can be lived by ordinary people; you just have to be that extra.

*Do not succumb to a world of familiarity and comfort;
be courageous enough to stand for something great with wonder.*

The small steps you take each day while focusing on your future will allow you to move closer toward your goals and conquer your fears.

Courage, faith, and integrity are put to the test when you follow through with what you stand for.

Todd A. Hyndman

Our true character is examined when we fall short of the person we were willing to become in the pursuit of our life's purpose.

Create a balanced, purposeful life—one that you care about and one that you are proud of.

Life is about the journey—so try harder, laugh, trust, be real, and truly live.

The world looks through troubled eyes, so don't be troubled by the eyes that are looking back at you.

Go full out and recreate life. See past the human condition to discover what is possible and live a life of abundance and strength.

Life is like skipping a rock across the water—you don't always know the direction or distance—you just have to be willing to throw and let go.

Great men are determined by courage and tested by faith.

The planned life breeds direction, but the unfocused life breeds misery. Which one awaits you?

*Life is like a revolving door—
you will go round and round until
you decide to step out.*

Our deepest fears are the very things we should move closer to. Avoidance stops growth right in its tracks.

Open your mouth wide—the world satisfies your appetite.

Our struggles are important because they keep us in check.

Move toward love. Do not run from it, no matter what the cost.

Make great things happen in your life that will lead to new opportunities, direction, and fulfillment.

As you make changes in your life, each new journey starts with hope, vision, and action.

Reach for your full potential,

because that is what God intended.

The authentic life we can experience is the one we embrace with passion, joy, and surrender.

You always have choices in life. Which choices are you making today to move you closer to the person you want to be?

Sometimes the uncomfortable things that happen to us are the very things we need to happen to us.

Good and bad things will happen in life, trust in the process and believe that everything happens for a reason.

The extent of what you want usually does not match up with what you need.

The important things in life tend to change the older we get. Life is all about cycles, peaks, and valleys. Embrace the change and reflect.

Growing pains create a space to find out who you are and what you are made of.

Life is staring you right in the face.

What do you tell it?

If life puzzles you, then become the person who will solve its mystery.

When things do not make sense anymore—stop, slow down, and trust that the meaning will be revealed. You will be glad you did.

One of our greatest achievements is to overcome our deepest fears.

The magical distance between your thoughts and your reality is your true courage.

Todd A. Hyndman

True friends are slow to judge,

eager to help, and willing to listen.

The beauty in life is enjoying the journey—so journey onward.

Who I am is all right with me, regardless whether or not you approve.

Make it a glorious moment—each and every moment—because glorious moments turn into beautiful and new beginnings.

Todd A. Hyndman

Life's adversities can bring out our greatest assets.

Life becomes exciting when you make things happen.

Push through the smoke and fog to see the horizon of your destiny.

Do not let failure become an option. Focus on becoming the person you were meant to be and shoot for success.

You must realize the potential within yourself to see the potential in others.

Let yourself rise, be proud, and take in all of life's wonderful blessings. Share your joy, and let the world know who you are.

The first step to transformation is the awareness that something in your life is out of balance and needs changing.

It is amazing what our lives can look like when we make the decision to become extraordinary and face our fears head on.

Account for something great in this world . . . kind of like leaving a mark—a mark of substance and excellence.

Life is too short to be ordinary, because you were born to be extraordinary.

Sometimes in life you expect things to go your way and they don't, but sometimes when you don't expect things to go your way, they do. The key is riding it through no matter what, embracing each day, and living in the moment.

The reality of your dreams is just one imagination away and one step forward into action.

Success or failure is determined by how you process your thoughts.

Life is too short not to go for it.

Purpose is something you seek and long for, but first you must pay attention and find it.

You will be doing yourself a disservice if you do not go after what it is you want in life. Follow your passion and use your fears to catapult you into action.

The ultimate goal is not true completion, but rather courage. Move forward with your initial vision and do something that you once thought was impossible.

From the past to the present, life brings us special moments. Each experience we can look forward to and reflect on.

See to it everyday that your life has no boundaries and is followed by many opportunities.

Our lives look so much brighter when we become extraordinary.

I would rather be happy than rich, healthy than famous, and true to myself than to be someone I am not.

Set your mind on being uncomfortable so you can see the world with new possibilities and hope.

Learn to open your mind and blaze your own trail. Understand what it means to find yourself once again, once anew.

Life should be about having fun—

plain and simple.

If you value yourself, find meaning to your life and go for it.

Not reaching your potential is like wanting to walk through quicksand.

Your troubles usually become as big as your mind makes them.

A small glimpse of a thought is lingering in the back of your subconscious mind. A memory, experience, or interaction can trigger it to rise to the surface. If you are in a creative space, magical things can happen—you might be surprised with the end result.

Happiness and peace will come your way if you focus on living in the moment. Not easy to do, but just continue to strive to embrace it.

Life is full of stumbles, but the key is to never stop getting up.

Life is a journey—different moments in time, new experiences, and new situations—some good and some bad. Learn as you go, feel, and get to know yourself better along the way, but never look back with regret.

You need to crawl before you can walk, walk before you can run, and run before you can fly.

And once you are flying, discover how it feels to soar.

Life is about people and making those special connections, networking, bonding, and sharing. Without people we could not survive, live, learn, and grow respectfully.

Quiet and stillness will give you strength if you listen and act accordingly. Simply listen to your heart rather than your mind, and you are on your way to peace and tranquility.

Great minds start with out-of-the-box thinking and a can-do attitude.

Seek a deeper meaning to your life and reflect on how you can make more of a positive impact for others in your community and the world. It all starts with inner growth and the right frame of mind.

Allow yourself to live your life's purpose. Listen to what your heart is saying and what your soul is feeling.

Shoot for the stars and run wild until you get there.

In order to have a new door open, you must trust in yourself and move forward.

You have to look beyond what is comfortable to see the opportunity.

If you rest on faith, expect the best, and assume greatness—your life can be extraordinary.

Perseverance is the bridge you must cross to reach success, but it requires belief and action.

It takes time, belief, and effort to become extraordinary.

If you have a genuine interest in others, they will open up and let you in.

Make up your mind to make your life matter.

You are worth every ounce of inspiration and imagination. You just have to believe it.

If you do what you love, you will experience balance, harmony, and freedom.

In order to take advantage of an opportunity, you must let go and move forward.

Allow yourself to transform into the brilliant person you were meant to be, because brilliance creates vision and creativity.

If you know what you are looking for in life, be sure you look in the right places.

Life will lead you down a road somewhere. If it becomes painful, how long are you willing to stay there?

Your life is always an open book; you can write your own chapters at any time. Do you want others to read your story?

Some things you cannot change, you just have to accept them and trust the journey.

Progress starts when you recognize your fears, put one foot in front of the other, and trust that you will cross the finish line.

We grow the most when we are in the valley, and have faith that we are soon to see a peak.

This road of life we travel has bumps, curves, potholes, and road blocks. However, this does not deter us from keeping our eyes on the road and our hands on the wheel. Life's lessons teach us how to prepare for obstacles.

It is better to experience a fruitful life no matter what the cost, than to fear risk and be unhappy.

God wants us to take risks and to live courageously.

Sometimes life is like having a set of braces on your teeth. It hurts, it's uncomfortable, and you go through changes and challenges until things get straightened out.

Walking through the eye of the storm with acceptance and peace will get you one step closer to stillness.

If you want to experience personal growth, ask God to stretch you.

Live boldly so that others may follow your example.

The measure of a person is not determined by money, fame, or possessions, but rather how he or she cares for family and acts toward others.

Bridge the gap between negative thinking and achieving your possibilities, one action step at a time.

Once you become true to your authentic self, you might just find the person wanting to spend their life with you.

We imagine, create, and make things happen with belief and perseverance. Our determination overrides doubt, and something extraordinary is born.

Great things are accomplished when you feel good about yourself.

Major changes start with small steps and a strong belief.

Positivity brings us purpose, one thought at a time.

The steps you make toward progress, growth, and a new life result from immediate action.

God wants us to see life through a clear lens.

Figure out what it is you want in life, and learn how to find it.

If you want your life to change—take a leap of faith, jump, and you will grow wings.

Those who want to succeed find a way to make it happen.

Achieving your life's purpose becomes easier with a road map. It will help you find your way even if you are lost.

Your legacy is built by your character; your character is built by your struggles, and your struggles keep you humbled. In that space you can see a glimpse of hope of the good that will come in the end.

Life happens when you wake up, think good thoughts, and say yes.

Ordinary lives can turn into extraordinary lives. You just have to turn on the power.

Infect the world with goodness.

Even when you don't know the outcome, all you need is the belief and the ability to try the unknown or the impossible.

The times when you are challenged and put to the test are when to look at your level of commitment. It will either allow you to push through or just stand still. You decide.

Learn how to slow down, say no, and choose a life of abundance.

Courage is finishing something you were willing to start.

ABOUT THE AUTHOR

Todd A. Hyndman has been encouraged from reading motivational quotes throughout his life. In December of 2009, he had an idea to write his own inspirational quote book. This project started to take on its own identity. Life Winks was born April of 2015.

www.ingramcontent.com/pod-product-compliance
Lightning Source LLC
Chambersburg PA
CBHW061330040426
42444CB00011B/2845